Original title:
Whispered Frost

Copyright © 2024 Swan Charm
All rights reserved.

Author: Aron Pilviste
ISBN HARDBACK: 978-9916-79-741-9
ISBN PAPERBACK: 978-9916-79-742-6
ISBN EBOOK: 978-9916-79-743-3

A Soft Frosting of Dreams

In the hush of night so deep,
Whispers of wishes softly creep.
Stars twinkle with a gentle gleam,
Painting sky with a soft dream.

Snowflakes dance on winter air,
Blanket earth with tender care.
Each flake holds a secret past,
Stories woven, shadows cast.

Moonlight spills on frozen ground,
In its glow, new hopes are found.
Silent wishes take their flight,
Borne on winds of chilly night.

Dreams arise like frosted lace,
Glimmers of a warmer place.
Hearts entwined in the soft glow,
In this magic, time moves slow.

With every breath, a tale is spun,
Underneath the silver sun.
A tapestry of dreams and fears,
Woven through the fleeting years.

Dreams Beneath the Ice

Silent wishes drift and glide,
Beneath the frozen, silver tide,
In the quiet, secrets lie,
Whispers captive, waiting nigh.

Fractured visions, pale and bright,
In crystal cages, caught in light,
They dance and shimmer, soft and rare,
Trapped in time, suspended air.

A world of wonder, veiled and cold,
Stories waiting to be told,
In frosty dreams, hope takes flight,
Beneath the watchful winter's night.

Silent echoes, soft embrace,
Yearning for a warm, sweet place,
Beneath the ice, the heart does trust,
In frosty realms, we find our lust.

Emerge anew when springtime calls,
As sunlight breaks the frozen walls,
Dreams beneath the ice will rise,
To touch the stars, to paint the skies.

Whirls of Frost

Whirls of frost dance in the air,
Delicate patterns, cold and rare,
Each flake whispers, soft and light,
Twinkling like stars in the night.

Brittle branches wear their gowns,
Encrusted jewels, diamond crowns,
Nature's breath, a frozen song,
In frigid waltz, we all belong.

Waves of chill sweep through the trees,
Carried on the winter's breeze,
In swirling masses, spirits twine,
Whirls of frost, a grand design.

Glimmers bright on fields of white,
A world transformed, a canvas bright,
In each swirl, a memory kept,
In frosty dreams, we've gently stepped.

Breathe in deep the frosty air,
A crisp embrace, beyond compare,
In whirls of frost, we find our peace,
As winter's magic does not cease.

The Gentle Hold of Ice

In the hush of a winter morn,
The world lies still, soft and worn,
The gentle hold of ice around,
Wraps us in peace, a quiet sound.

Crystalline blankets cover ground,
Silent whispers where dreams are found,
Nature rests in frozen grace,
A moment held in love's embrace.

Each breath a cloud, a tender sigh,
As snowflakes fall from a pastel sky,
Holding time in a fragile weave,
In this stillness, we believe.

Icicles hang like fragile art,
Adorning nature's beating heart,
In the gentle hold, we find our home,
Where even winter feels the warm roam.

With twilight's glow, the day slips by,
Holding dreams as the stars reply,
In winter's tender, softest clutch,
The hold of ice, a gentle touch.

Crystalline Whispers

Crystalline whispers fill the air,
Soft as secrets, light as prayer,
Each glimmer tells a tale untold,
Of winter nights and frosts so bold.

Voices echo in the frost,
Lingering moments never lost,
Through the branches, sounds do weave,
In the silence, hearts believe.

Fluttering forms of light ascend,
In their flight, our hopes do blend,
Crystalline dreams, a fleeting spark,
Illuminating pathways dark.

With every breath, the chill ignites,
Magic blooms in starry nights,
Whispers dance on winter's breath,
In crystal realms, we find our depth.

Unseen forces guide us still,
Through whispered dreams, the heart does thrill,
Crystalline whispers, soft and bright,
Beckon souls to chase the light.

The Caress of Winter's Breath

Whispers dance upon the breeze,
As frost-kissed air brings gentle ease.
Trees adorned in silver lace,
Time stands still in winter's grace.

The world wrapped in purest white,
Softly glows in fading light.
Echoes of the past so near,
Seasons change, but memories cheer.

From distant hills, the chill arrives,
In silence, nature's heart survives.
Each flake speaks a tale once told,
In winter's arms, the dreams unfold.

Secrets in the Silent Snow

A hush blankets the sleeping earth,
Each flake a witness to rebirth.
Beneath the veil, a world concealed,
Whispers dwell, softly revealed.

Footprints mark the paths we've flown,
Stories hidden, yet well-known.
In every drift, a secret lies,
As winter weaves its ancient ties.

Moonlight glimmers on the pale,
Casting shadows that tell a tale.
In unity, the night holds tight,
Wrapped in dreams, bathed in light.

Shadows of a Frozen Dream

In the stillness of the night,
Frozen dreams take silent flight.
Haunting echoes softly call,
In twilight's glow, we find it all.

Figures dance in glimmering white,
Lost in pathways of soft light.
The chill wraps our hearts so tight,
As whispers fade into the night.

A tapestry of shadowed sleep,
In winter's grasp, we drift and leap.
Through silvered pines, we wander free,
Lost within the reverie.

The Quietude of Winter's Hold

The world slows in a graceful hush,
As winter melds the dawn's soft blush.
Each breath a cloud in frosty air,
Moments linger, calm and rare.

Branches heavy with snowy crowns,
Nature dons her crystal gowns.
In quietude, we find our peace,
Letting go, our cares release.

Close your eyes and feel the chill,
In stillness, hear the world stand still.
Wrapped in warmth of heart and home,
Through winter's reign, together roam.

Glacial Whispers of Time

In the stillness of the night,
Frosty echoes softly gleam,
Time flows slowly, pure and bright,
Captured in a frozen dream.

Whispers weave through silver trees,
Glistening like stars up high,
Gentle breath of winter's freeze,
Tells the tales that never die.

Snowflakes dance on winter's breath,
Spirals twirl in soft embrace,
Nature's sigh transcends to death,
Yet life lingers in this place.

Stillness holds the fleeting hour,
Moments freeze, then drift away,
Time creates a frosted flower,
Petals fading into gray.

Every flake a memory,
Bound in cold, forever tied,
Glacial whispers set me free,
In this chill, I bide my ride.

Silence Draped in Winter's Grace

Snowflakes fall like whispers sweet,
Blanketing the world in white,
Silence wraps us in its sheet,
Holding close the soft twilight.

Trees stand tall with branches bare,
Crystalline against the sky,
Frozen beauty everywhere,
In this hush, our spirits fly.

Each breath visible and bright,
Dancing in the frosty air,
Moments caught in purest light,
Winter's essence, beyond compare.

Footsteps leave a tender trace,
Marking paths where silence dwells,
In the chill of winter's grace,
Nature weaves her secret spells.

Stillness reigns, the world at peace,
Embraced by the cold and calm,
In this pause, our worries cease,
Winter's love, a gentle balm.

The Soft Kiss of Icebound Dreams

Dreams encapsulated in frost,
Glimmers dancing on the ground,
In this cold, we count the cost,
Of the warmth we never found.

Moonlight weaves through snowy lanes,
Softly kissing every tree,
Echoes linger, sweet refrains,
In this place, we long to be.

Frozen rivers gently flow,
Carving paths through icy lands,
In their depths, our hopes aglow,
Guided by the winter's hands.

Whispers of a world asleep,
Cradled in the cold embrace,
In the silence, echoes seep,
Fleeting time, a soft caress.

Icebound dreams take flight tonight,
Swirling in a silent dance,
Wrapped in layers, pure and white,
Winter gives us one last chance.

Silent Shivers

Chill settles in the air, crisp,
Fingers numb in winter's clutch,
Stillness wraps the night, a lisp,
Softly urging us to touch.

Breath of frost on window panes,
Whispers brush the peaceful night,
Every shimmer holds its chains,
Binding dreams in purest light.

Gentle shivers roam the land,
Blanket warm, we seek to find,
Nature's voice, a guiding hand,
In this quiet, souls unwind.

Stars emerge in velvet hue,
Guiding hearts to find their way,
Silent shivers, fresh and new,
Offering the world to play.

In the hush, we close our eyes,
Embracing every icy gleam,
Silent whispers, soft goodbyes,
Turn our dreams to winter's dream.

Glistening Secrets Revealed

In the shadow of the night,
Whispers dance in silver light.
Stars above, like eyes that see,
Secrets shared, wild and free.

Through the trees, a soft breeze stirs,
Ancient tales in tangled spurs.
Misty fog wraps the still air,
Glistening dreams without a care.

Beneath the moon's warm, tender gaze,
Hidden paths and secret ways.
Frozen whispers float and twirl,
As silence wraps the sleeping world.

With every flicker, stories bloom,
Shadows flicker, dispel gloom.
Nature's heart beats strong and true,
Beneath the sky, a vibrant hue.

In this realm where secrets blend,
Life and magic softly mend.
Glistening truths, now revealed,
In the night's embrace, concealed.

Veils of Ice

A world adorned in crystal lace,
Nature's pause, a frozen grace.
Each breath hangs in the chilled air,
Beauty dwells in silence rare.

Beneath the sky, so vast and bright,
Veils of ice reflect the light.
Softly whispering, the wind calls,
Echoes dance in winter's thrall.

Trees wear coats of frosty sheen,
Every branch a sparkling dream.
Footsteps muffled, hearts grow still,
In this realm where time stands still.

Snowflakes drift, a graceful flight,
Painting landscapes pure and white.
Every corner holds a night,
Veils of ice, a pure delight.

In this magic, find your peace,
Let the winter's chaos cease.
Veils of ice, so gently spun,
Whisper tales of time undone.

The Quiet of the Frozen World

In the hush of winter's spell,
Echoes of the stillness dwell.
Snowflakes fall, a blanket deep,
In this silence, secrets sleep.

Trees stand tall, their branches bare,
Kissed by frost, a crystal flare.
Nature pauses, breath imbued,
In this calm, a quietude.

Footprints trace a path so rare,
Wander softly, without care.
Every sigh, a whispered word,
In the quiet, hearts are stirred.

When the night wraps all in gray,
Stars emerge to light the way.
Dreams take flight on evening's wing,
In the frozen world, we sing.

So find your peace where cold winds blow,
In this kingdom of frost and snow.
The quiet holds a beauty rare,
A frozen world beyond compare.

A Soft Winter's Breath

Gentle whispers on the breeze,
Rustle through the barren trees.
A soft breath, winter's sigh,
Quotes from nature, low and high.

The ground is crisp beneath my feet,
Every step, a rhythmic beat.
Softly falls the evening's light,
Streetlamps gleam, a warm invite.

Chilled air dances on my skin,
Echoes of warmth lie deep within.
Under stars that twinkle bright,
In this calm, my heart takes flight.

As shadows stretch, a quiet scene,
Nature wraps the world in sheen.
A soft winter, calm and slow,
Where peace and wonder freely flow.

Let the chill embrace surround,
In this moment, love is found.
A soft winter's breath draws near,
Whispered dreams, crystal clear.

The Quiet Serenade of Snow

Softly it falls, a gentle dance,
Covering earth in a white expanse.
Muted whispers fill the air,
As winter's breath, a calm affair.

Trees stand tall in glistening grace,
Blankets of snow, a fleeting trace.
Footprints linger, then disappear,
In the hush, the world feels near.

The sky dons a cloak of silver light,
Stars twinkle softly, a wondrous sight.
Crystals shimmer in the moon's glow,
A fairy tale in the silent show.

Each flake unique, a fragile art,
Nature whispers secrets to the heart.
In this stillness, one finds peace,
As magic weaves, and troubles cease.

Enigma of the Shimmering Chill

The air is crisp, a whispered tune,
Beneath the gaze of the silver moon.
Icicles hang like delicate dreams,
Reflecting the world in frozen beams.

Frosty patterns on window panes,
Nature's artistry that never wanes.
A shiver runs down the spine,
As shadows dance with secrets divine.

In every corner, a mystery lies,
Echoes of laughter, distant sighs.
Footsteps crunch on the frosted ground,
A haunting melody, profound.

Veils of cold hold stories untold,
Each flake a wish, a memory bold.
Under the blanket of winter's embrace,
We find our dreams in a frosty space.

Ethereal Frosty Whispers

Whispers of frost kiss the trees,
Swaying gently in the breeze.
A world transformed, so serene,
Wrapped in layers of crystallized sheen.

Silvery strands weave through the night,
As stars above shine with delight.
The moon spills secrets on the land,
In an icy grip, a gentle hand.

Every breath is a cloud, so light,
In the stillness, a soft twilight.
Muffled sounds through the frosty air,
Replace the din with nature's prayer.

Cosmic dreams in a frozen space,
Invite us to linger, to embrace.
With every glance, a wonder reveals,
As the heart dances, the spirit heals.

Midnight Glimmers of Ice

Under the cover of starlit skies,
Glimmers of ice hold silent cries.
Each sparkle tells a tale untold,
Of distant lands and dreams of old.

The world adorned in twinkling white,
Sways gently in the soft moonlight.
Frozen lakes reflect the night,
Embracing darkness, pure and bright.

In shadows, echoes weave a song,
A symphony where all belong.
Every hush and shiver, a treat,
As winter weaves her magic sweet.

Late night whispers through the trees,
Emphasized by the mellow breeze.
Here in the glimmers, we find our rest,
In the heart of winter, truly blessed.

Breaths of an Icy Dawn

The morning breathes a crystal chill,
Nature's stillness, a frozen thrill.
Sunlight whispers through the trees,
Casting shadows with a gentle breeze.

Hushed are footsteps on the snow,
Where dreams of warmth begin to flow.
Each frost-laden branch bows low,
A winter's grace in soft-glow.

The world adorned in white attire,
Each breath a moment to inspire.
Frozen lakes reflect the skies,
A masterpiece where beauty lies.

Birds flit by, with hearts aglow,
Chirping songs of winsome flow.
In this realm, where silence reigns,
Life persists amid the chains.

Glimmers burst as dawn unfolds,
A canvas vast, with hues of gold.
Embrace the chill, let worries flee,
In icy dawn, find harmony.

Glimmering Secrets of the Blizzard

Whirling snowflakes dance above,
Whispers hidden, gently shove.
The blizzard's grip, both fierce and kind,
Secrets buried, intertwined.

Underneath the roaring storm,
Silent tales take unique form.
Glimmering shards of mysteries,
Nature's veil, her histories.

Frosted windows, tales untold,
Glittering stories, brave and bold.
A world transformed into a dream,
Where winter's essence softly gleams.

Beneath the snow, life sleeps tight,
Awaiting spring's return to light.
Each gust reveals a fleeting truth,
In frozen breath, we find our youth.

Through the tempest, hearts grow clear,
In the blizzard, we have no fear.
Glimmering secrets gently weave,
In winter's heart, we learn to believe.

Veiled in Serene Stillness

In quiet woods, a veil descends,
Where time stands still, the world mends.
Snowflakes settle, soft and light,
A blanket hushes day and night.

Branches draped in icy lace,
Nature whispers, finds her grace.
Each flake falls like a silent prayer,
Wrapped in warmth, love fills the air.

The frozen pond, a mirror bright,
Echoes dreams in soft twilight.
Reflections dance, a fleeting chance,
To glimpse the peace in winter's glance.

Each breath is a soft lullaby,
Beneath the stars, as night draws nigh.
Serene stillness, a sacred space,
Where the heart shall find its place.

In this haven, worries cease,
Embracing calm, a gentle peace.
Veiled in stillness, spirits soar,
In winter's arms, forevermore.

Tread Softly, Frozen Ground

Tread softly on this frosted way,
Where whispers linger, come what may.
Each step a crunch, a story told,
As morning sun turns silver to gold.

Beneath the snow, secrets lie,
In every flake that drifts from sky.
Nature's canvas, pure and bright,
Invites us forth, ignites our sight.

The world awaits with bated breath,
In frozen stillness, life and death.
Tread lightly, for the ground's a song,
Whispering truths, both weak and strong.

In the dance of winter's chill,
Feel the magic, embrace the thrill.
With every step, the earth responds,
In frozen moments, the heart absconds.

So wander here, with wonder found,
In the splendor of this frozen ground.
Let each footfall hold a sigh,
In winter's grasp, let spirits fly.

Veiled in Crystal Dreams

In the realm of shadows, whispers dive,
Where fragile hopes and wishes thrive.
Glistening patterns weave the night,
A dance of dreams, a silver light.

Softly glows the moonlit haze,
Casting spells of secret gaze.
Every shimmer tells a tale,
Through crystal paths, our hearts set sail.

Broken promises drift like mist,
In this fairytale, none are missed.
Stars above like diamonds gleam,
All wrapped within a crystal dream.

Floating thoughts like clouds of white,
Journeying forth, lost in flight.
A fleeting moment, a soft sigh,
In the crystal dreams, we learn to fly.

Night unfolds its velvet grace,
In every corner, a hidden space.
Veiled in calm, we find our way,
In crystal dreams, forever stay.

Frostbitten Secrets in the Air

Cold winds whisper through the trees,
Carrying tales with chilling ease.
Frostbitten secrets ride the breeze,
In this wintry world, nature freezes.

Every breath becomes a ghost,
Silent echoes of what matters most.
In the stillness, hearts conspire,
To reveal truths that we desire.

Icicles hang like swords of glass,
Reflecting shadows as they pass.
In this realm where time stands still,
We chase the whispers, bend to will.

Underneath the frozen moon,
Secrets linger, a haunting tune.
With every frost, the stories grow,
Of love and loss wrapped in the snow.

As dawn approaches, colors stir,
Awakening dreams that softly blur.
Frostbitten secrets softly slide,
In the air, our fears collide.

Echoes of the Frostbound Heart

Beneath the frost, our hearts reside,
Locked away where feelings hide.
Echoes linger in the cold,
Whispers of stories yet untold.

Time drips slowly like the dew,
Each moment precious, yet so few.
Fragile bonds that weather fate,
In this silence, love can wait.

A heart encased in icy chains,
Longing for warmth amidst the pains.
Through the chill, we seek the flame,
In each echo, love calls our name.

Snowflakes dance upon the ground,
Painting silence, a gentle sound.
Frostbound hearts entwined as one,
In echoes, love's promise begun.

With the thaw, new hopes will rise,
Beneath the sun, a brighter guise.
In the warmth, our souls will part,
To share the echoes of the heart.

Twilight's Cold Embrace

At the edge of day, shadows creep,
In twilight's fold, the world will sleep.
Chill of night wraps all around,
In quiet moments, peace is found.

Stars awaken, bright and bold,
In the darkness, secrets unfold.
Twilight whispers, tales of yore,
Of icy dreams on distant shore.

Each breath whispered in the night,
Flickering softly, candlelight.
In the stillness, time stands still,
Embracing shadows, bending will.

Through twilight's lens, we softly gaze,
In the chill, our hearts ablaze.
With every sigh, the world finds grace,
Engulfed in twilight's cold embrace.

As dawn approaches, colors blend,
The chill of night begins to end.
In warmth's caress, we find our place,
Eternal echo of twilight's grace.

The Gentle Pull of Winter's Breath

In the hush of the evening glow,
Softly falls the silent snow.
Whispers of the pine trees sway,
Winter calls the heart to play.

Candles flicker, shadows long,
Echoes of a distant song.
Cozy warmth from fireside cheer,
Embrace the chill, hold loved ones near.

Frozen lakes, a silver sheet,
Footsteps crunch, a cold retreat.
Nature pauses, breath held tight,
As stars pierce the velvet night.

In every flake, a tale untold,
Stories of the brave and bold.
Beneath the moon's soft, gentle light,
Winter's breath ignites the night.

Enchanted in a Frosty Lattice

Glistening branches, a frozen dream,
Nature weaves her icy seam.
Lattice work in silver bright,
Glistening in the soft moonlight.

Footsteps trace a wondrous path,
In the cold, a gentle laugh.
Frost adorns each branch and leaf,
Winter's art, a grand motif.

Stars above like diamonds shine,
In the air, the taste of brine.
Magical hues of lavender,
Dance like spirits, light and pure.

Whispers carried on the breeze,
Nature's wonders, soft and free.
In this place, we lose our care,
Enchanted by the frosty air.

Crystal Whispers in the Night

Beneath the sky, where shadows creep,
The world lies still, in gentle sleep.
Frosted whispers, a silent song,
Night wraps softly, all night long.

Stars like crystals twinkle bright,
Guiding dreams through endless night.
Each breath comes slow, a frosty sigh,
In the hush, the heart will fly.

Moonbeams lace the sleeping ground,
Painting peace in softest sound.
In the dark, a world reborn,
As the winter sky is worn.

Time stands still, a moment rare,
In the magic of the air.
All creation holds its breath,
In the silence, life finds depth.

Shards of Frosty Reverie

As dawn breaks on a crystal morn,
A world anew, softly reborn.
Shards of ice catch the light,
Sparkling dreams in colors bright.

Every tree, a work of art,
Nature's grace plays its part.
Rays of sun through frosty glass,
Time slows down, moments pass.

The air is crisp, a breath of cheer,
Frozen echoes, crystal clear.
Voices dance on winter's breeze,
Whispers carried through the trees.

In this land of white delight,
Magic thrives in morning light.
Each twinkle holds a secret true,
In frosty reveries, we renew.

Soft Shadows of Winter

The snowflakes fall, gentle and light,
Covering the earth, a silvery white.
In soft shadows, the world seems to pause,
Whispers of peace, nature's own cause.

Trees bend low, cloaked in cold grace,
Quiet moments in a frozen space.
Breath turns to mist in the chilled air,
Winter's embrace, tender and rare.

The sun dips low, a warm golden hue,
Painting the skies in a tranquil blue.
As night descends, stars twinkle bright,
Guiding our hearts through the quiet night.

Footsteps leave prints in the soft, white snow,
A journey begins where stillness flows.
With each gentle breeze, stories are spun,
Soft shadows embrace the setting sun.

The Embrace of Stillness

In the heart of winter, silence reigns,
Wrapped in soft blankets, nature sustains.
Gentle is the touch of the frost-kissed air,
A moment to breathe, to savor, to care.

The world slows down, in time's gentle hold,
Whispers of wisdom in stories untold.
Trees stand tall, stoic yet kind,
Embracing the stillness, a peace we find.

Moonlight dances on the frozen streams,
Softly illuminating our fleeting dreams.
Within this quiet, hearts seek to know,
The beauty of stillness, as soft winds blow.

Footprints in snow tell of journeys past,
Echoes of laughter, memories that last.
Wrapped in the stillness, we pause to feel,
The gentle embrace, the world healed and real.

Frozen Whispers of Time

Time stands still in the winter's breath,
Frozen whispers speak of life and death.
Each flake that falls is a memory spun,
Fragile and fleeting, yet full of fun.

The chill in the air carries secrets untold,
Stories of ages, both new and old.
Each gust of wind sings a song so sweet,
Of moments forgotten, where journeys meet.

Icicles glisten in the soft morning light,
Reminding us gently of the long winter night.
With every heartbeat, the seasons align,
In the dance of existence, a rhythm divine.

As shadows grow long, the sky turns to gray,
Fleeting and fragile, each moment in play.
Frozen whispers of time softly call,
Holding our hearts, together we fall.

Twilight's Frosty Kiss

At dusk the world wears a diamond glow,
Twilight whispers secrets only stars know.
A frosty kiss brushes over the land,
In the stillness of night, we dream hand in hand.

Cool air wraps around like a gentle embrace,
Reflecting the magic of time and space.
With every heartbeat, the silence sings,
Promising wonders that winter brings.

Crickets hum softly beneath the pale moon,
As night pulls the curtain, stars dance in tune.
Each twinkle a promise of hopes intertwined,
In twilight's soft grasp, our spirits aligned.

The frost paints the world in a glistening hue,
As moments together bloom fresh as the dew.
In the quiet of night, love's warmth will stay,
In twilight's embrace, we softly drift away.

The Quiet Dance of Winter

Softly falls the snow at night,
Whispers wrap the world in white.
Branches bow with gentle grace,
Time stands still in this embrace.

Footsteps hush on frosted ground,
Nature's song is all around.
A silent symphony we hear,
As winter's breath whispers near.

Stars above in endless glow,
Guide the falling flakes below.
Each breath taken feels like art,
Painting dreams within the heart.

Fires crackle, shadows dance,
In this tranquil, snowy trance.
Every flake a love letter,
Winter's soft embrace, a fetter.

Where cold meets the warmth of light,
In the quiet of the night.
A frosty world, serene, divine,
In winter's grace, our souls entwine.

A Melody of Snowflakes

Each snowflake falls, a crafted tune,
Softly kissing the earth, a boon.
They swirl and twirl, a graceful dance,
Inviting all to take a chance.

Nature hums a gentle song,
As winter's heart beats pure and strong.
With every flake, a story spun,
A melody of cold begun.

Beneath the moon's soft, silvery glow,
Invited are we to wander slow.
Each moment holds a spark of light,
In the hush of a winter night.

Whispers weave through frozen air,
A silence deep, beyond compare.
Frosted branches sway with ease,
Nature's chorus in the breeze.

In the stillness, hope is found,
As snowflakes blanket all around.
Their fragile dance, a fleeting sight,
In winter's arms, we find delight.

Winter's Fragile Note

A fragile note is softly played,
Upon the strings of winter's shade.
Each whisper carries tales untold,
In the chill of nights so cold.

Crystal patterns lace the trees,
A testament to winter's freeze.
The world transforms in quiet light,
A canvas brightened by the night.

Voices hushed, the air stands still,
Echoes linger on the hill.
Every flake a wish, a prayer,
Winter's magic fills the air.

Gentle winds weave through the pines,
As shadows dance on snowy lines.
In fragile beauty, dreams take flight,
A symphony of pure delight.

Time slows down, the moment glows,
Wrapped in blankets, warmth bestows.
Each breath whispers winter's grace,
In this serene, enchanted space.

A Shiver of Silence

In the stillness, silence creaks,
A shiver dances, softly speaks.
Frosty fingers trace the ground,
Every breath a whispered sound.

Shadows stretch beneath the moon,
Winter sings a gentle tune.
Stars above in quiet gleam,
Weaving through a nighttime dream.

Frozen branches, soft as lace,
Embrace the night with tender grace.
Every moment, pure and rare,
A shiver whispers, linger there.

Chill of air, warmth in the heart,
Every flake a work of art.
Nature's calm is felt within,
In this silence, we begin.

As dawn breaks, a golden hue,
The world awakens, fresh and new.
Yet in the quiet, we still find,
A shiver of silence, beautifully kind.

Glistening Hushes

Moonlight falls in silent grace,
Whispers dance in empty space.
Stars above begin to glow,
Wrapped in peace, the world moves slow.

Gentle frost on blades of green,
Nature's magic, softly seen.
Every breath is crisp and clear,
Hushed reflections draw us near.

Night enfolds the earth so tight,
Lanterns sparkle, purest light.
In this calm, our thoughts can drift,
In the quiet, hearts can lift.

Softly now, the shadows play,
Creeping gently, night to day.
In this moment, time we share,
Glistening hushes everywhere.

Wrapped in dreams, we feel the glow,
In this stillness, love will flow.
Whispers linger, soft as air,
In the calm, we find our care.

Chilled Echoes

In the fog, the whispers call,
Through the night, they rise and fall.
Echoes dance on icy ground,
In their sweep, lost dreams are found.

Shadows blend with muted light,
Veils of silver hug the night.
Crimson leaves upon the frost,
In their beauty, we feel lost.

Frosty air brings tales anew,
Of forgotten moments, true.
As the silence wraps us tight,
Chilled echoes fill the night.

Moonbeams trace the pathways clear,
Guiding footsteps, drawing near.
In the still, we hear the past,
Moments fleeting, yet they last.

In the quiet, hearts align,
Timeless yearning, softly shine.
Through the chill of winter's breath,
Echoes linger, dance with death.

Frosted Murmurs

The world wraps in a shimm'ring sheet,
Footsteps soft and pure, discreet.
Frosted murmurs softly sigh,
Underneath the pale, blue sky.

Crystal branches, tales they weave,
In every whisper, hearts believe.
Nature hums a secret tune,
Beneath the watchful, silver moon.

The chill awakens dreams so bright,
In the depths of winter's night.
Voices linger on the breeze,
Frosted murmurs, sweet as these.

With each breath, the magic grows,
Softly glowing in the snows.
In this realm, our spirits dance,
Frosted dreams, a lovely trance.

Moments freeze, yet time moves on,
In this hush, we're never gone.
Frosted echoes, light as air,
In these murmurs, we find care.

Beneath the Icy Veil

Whispers cradle the quiet night,
Beneath the veil, the world feels right.
Icy tendrils softly creep,
In this hush, our secrets keep.

Shimmering shadows softly glint,
In each silence, thoughts imprint.
Glacial dreams weave through the air,
Peace enveloped in frosted care.

As the stars begin to gleam,
Every heartbeat carries dream.
Underneath the blanket white,
Hope arises in the night.

Moments linger, sweetly bold,
In the frosty, darkened cold.
Beneath the icy veil we find,
The warmth of love, forever kind.

Together wrapped in fate's sweet hand,
We embrace this frozen land.
In the depths, our spirits soar,
Beneath the veil, forever more.

The Sigh of Icy Winds

In the hush of midnight's glow,
Whispers dance where cold winds blow.
Trees stand tall in frosted white,
Dreams take flight on wings of night.

Moonlit paths, a silver thread,
Footsteps soft where spirits tread.
Echoes linger, shadows blend,
Time stands still as sorrows mend.

Crystal clouds in twilight breathe,
Nature's breath a graceful wreath.
Silent pleas in frosty air,
Hope emerges, bright and rare.

Beneath the stars, the world is hushed,
In winter's grasp, the hearts are crushed.
Yet in the chill, a warmth resides,
A flame ignites where love abides.

In every sigh, a tale unfolds,
Of ancient dreams and secrets told.
The icy winds, they softly call,
A serenade to us all.

Hushed Crystals on Silent Ground

Glistening gems 'neath moonlit skies,
Awake the world with quiet sighs.
Each crystal shard, a story told,
In frosty nights, their magic unfolds.

Snowflakes fall, a gentle grace,
Kissing earth with a tender embrace.
Nature sleeps in a dreamy trance,
As shadows weave a winter dance.

Footsteps crunch upon the ice,
Whispers drift, a soft entice.
The beauty lies in silence found,
In hushed crystals on silent ground.

A blanket white, so pure and deep,
Holding secrets that we keep.
In every flake, a tranquil sound,
Hushed crystals weave the night around.

As dawn awakens, colors blend,
Winter's chill begins to end.
Yet in this time, a stillness stays,
In hushed crystals, time delays.

Winter's Veiled Lullaby

Softly sung in whispers low,
Winter's lullaby begins to flow.
Blankets warm, the hearth aglow,
Dreams carry on where winds do blow.

Stars alight in velvet night,
Crimson embers, a flickering light.
The world pauses, cradled in peace,
As nature sings her sweet release.

Frosted branches, a silken veil,
Stories linger in the gale.
Under stars, we hear the sound,
Of winter's song, so profound.

Time drifts softly like the snow,
In this moment, all is slow.
In echoes of the night so spry,
We find solace in the sky.

Embrace the chill with open arms,
Winter's lullaby holds us in charms.
In gentle dreams, let spirits lie,
For peace awaits where shadows fly.

A Breath of Frozen Silence

In the stillness, moments freeze,
Winter's breath whispers through the trees.
A canvas white, untouched and pure,
Nature's stillness: our hearts endure.

Icy fingers trace the ground,
A cloak of frost, a magic found.
Footprints vanish, the world unknown,
In frozen silence, true peace is sown.

Stars twinkle in the endless night,
Guiding souls with their gentle light.
Wrapped in whispers, soft and deep,
In this quiet, secrets keep.

Every breath, a cloud of mist,
Memories shimmer, too sweet to resist.
In this hallowed, sacred space,
Frozen silence grants us grace.

As dawn approaches, hues will shift,
But in this breath, our spirits lift.
A dance of cold, a warmth divine,
In frozen silence, hearts align.

Frost-kissed Secrets

Whispers in the chill of night,
Moonlight dances, soft and bright.
Hidden dreams in silence tread,
Frost-kissed secrets softly spread.

Beneath the stars, the world sleeps light,
Each breath a cloud, a fleeting sight.
In stillness deep, the shadows play,
Veils of frost, where spirits sway.

Shimmering layers, stories weave,
Nature's tapestry, we believe.
Glistening paths that time won't fade,
In frozen grace, we serenade.

Crisp air bites, yet warmth will find,
A gentle touch, love intertwined.
In every flake, a tale to share,
Frost-kissed secrets linger rare.

Awakened hearts in winter's grasp,
Together we hold, a cherished clasp.
In quiet joy, beneath the skies,
Frost-kissed dreams that never die.

Icicle Serenade

Hanging high from rooftops' edge,
Chimes of ice on winter's ledge.
Glistening clear in morning's light,
Icicle serenade, pure delight.

They sway with whispers, soft and low,
Melodies of frost that flow.
In the air, a crystal song,
Icicles hum, where dreams belong.

Underneath the boughs of pine,
Winter's breath feels so divine.
Nature's orchestra, cold yet warm,
Icicle notes, a charming charm.

With every drip, a drop of glee,
Echoes of the wild, so free.
A symphony, both bold and bright,
Icicle serenade, pure delight.

In the twilight, colors blend,
Frozen moments never end.
Together we listen and sang,
To the sound of ice that rang.

Silent Snowfall

In the hush of the falling snow,
World transforms in a gentle glow.
Each flake descends with quiet grace,
Silent snowfall, a soft embrace.

Pine trees wear their white attire,
Blankets of peace, our hearts inspire.
Whispers drift through the frosty air,
Silent snowfall, beyond compare.

Footsteps muffled in nature's quilt,
As dreams awaken, no guilt.
Winter's breath, a tender sigh,
Silent snowfall, a lullaby.

Stars peek through in the velvet night,
Guiding wanderers with their light.
In the stillness, we find our role,
Silent snowfall, a healing soul.

Hold this moment in your heart,
As we cherish this winter's art.
In frosted beauty, joy will grow,
Silent snowfall, pure and slow.

Gentle Crystalisations

Delicate shapes in the morning sun,
Gentle crystallisations have begun.
Nature's jewels in still repose,
A tapestry where beauty flows.

Frosted branches wear their crown,
In the mist, no hint of frown.
A quiet grace on every bough,
Gentle crystallisations show us how.

Glistening pathways, a wonderland,
Each step taken, magic at hand.
Sparkling dreams weave through the air,
Gentle crystallisations everywhere.

The air, crisp, holds stories untold,
Of winter's whispers, soft and bold.
As we wander, hearts align,
Gentle crystallisations, so divine.

In frosty breaths and laughter shared,
In every moment, we are ensnared.
With love as our guide, let's explore,
Gentle crystallisations, forevermore.

Secrets of the Winter Breeze

In the hush of the winter glow,
Whispers travel soft and low.
Bearing tales from the frozen trees,
Carried gently on the breeze.

Footsteps crunch on the layered snow,
Follow where the cold winds blow.
Silent secrets in the air,
Winter's quiet, everywhere.

Stars twinkle in the night's embrace,
While the frost leaves a silver trace.
In this calm, a world transforms,
In the midst of winter's storms.

Moments wrapped in frosty lace,
Nature's beauty, a silent grace.
The breath of winter, sweet and dear,
Whispers that only hearts can hear.

Beneath the moon, shadows play,
As night wraps the world in gray.
Every flake, a whispered thought,
In the quiet, peace is sought.

Frigid Whispers

The air is sharp, the silence deep,
Embraced by night, the world in sleep.
Frigid whispers kiss the ground,
In their touch, a magic found.

Snowflakes dance like fleeting dreams,
Clinging to the world as it seems.
Each breath drawn a frosty sigh,
In the shadows, the echoes lie.

Moonlight glimmers on icy streams,
Reflecting all our quiet themes.
Nature's soft, unnoticed song,
Frigid, yet where we belong.

Underneath a chilling haze,
The world sparkles in a daze.
Frosty branches, gnarled and old,
Holding stories yet untold.

In the stillness, secrets blend,
Whispers loop and twist and bend.
Frigid dreams take flight anew,
In the heart of winter's hue.

The Quiet Chill

The quiet chill wraps the night,
Embracing all in soft respite.
Breath of winter, crisp and clear,
Echoes linger, drawing near.

Moonlit paths in silver shine,
Nature's canvas, pure, divine.
Frosty whispers tease the air,
Each moment a delicate prayer.

Branches bow with a gentle grace,
While shadows dance in a still place.
Coldness cradles every thought,
In the peace that winter brought.

Stars peer down like whispers soft,
Guiding dreams that lift aloft.
In the dark, the world holds still,
Wrapped in nature's quiet thrill.

Time slows down in this embrace,
Every second, a gentle trace.
In the corner of the night,
The quiet chill brings forth delight.

Murmured Icicles

Murmured icicles hang with grace,
Framing winter's cold embrace.
Dripping secrets, soft and clear,
Frozen melodies we hear.

Underneath the arching sky,
Frosted wonders close and high.
Every drop, a whispered tale,
Glittering like a silver scale.

Crisp air fills the silent space,
While shadows weave a gentle lace.
Winter's breath, a soothing balm,
In its grasp, a timeless calm.

Icicles glisten, sharp and bright,
Holding shadows in the light.
Nature speaks in tones so low,
In this chill, our hearts will glow.

Fractured light in colors blend,
In their beauty, sorrows mend.
Murmured whispers, soft and sweet,
In winter's arms, we find our feet.

Serenity in Winter's Embrace

Silence wraps the world in white,
Snowflakes dance in gentle flight.
The trees stand tall, their branches bare,
Nature whispers, a tranquil prayer.

Footsteps crunch on crisp, cold ground,
In this stillness, peace is found.
The air is clear, the sky so blue,
Winter's touch, a soothing hue.

The hearth glows bright within our home,
Warmth surrounds as we softly roam.
A cup of cocoa warms our hands,
Together we weave life's simple plans.

As twilight falls, the colors blend,
The day retreats, the night ascends.
Stars peek through the velvet sky,
In winter's arms, we softly sigh.

In this embrace, we find our grace,
Every moment, a tender trace.
With every breath, joy intersects,
Serenity in winter reflects.

Frosty Morning Murmurs

Morning breaks with frost so bright,
Nature sparkles in the light.
Birds awake with gentle calls,
Echoes dance through winter's halls.

The air is crisp, the world aglow,
Each step reveals a hidden show.
Pine trees wear their frosty crowns,
Life awakens in icy gowns.

Sunrise paints the sky with gold,
Stories of warmth in shadows told.
Breath of life in frozen air,
A moment's stillness, pure and rare.

Streams whisper beneath the ice,
Nature's song, a silent vice.
Each crystal bead, a tale to share,
Frosty magic fills the air.

A world reborn in winter's hold,
The beauty found in the cold.
With every sigh, the heart will stir,
In frosty morns, sweet murmurs blur.

Flickers of an Icebound Night

Night descends with a silver sheen,
Stars alight in a canvas keen.
Moonlight glimmers on the frost,
In this beauty, no warmth is lost.

Leaves whisper with a brittle song,
In the stillness, we belong.
Shadows dance upon the snow,
Echoes of dreams begin to flow.

Each breath shows a misty trail,
Through the night, we softly sail.
The chill wraps tightly around our skin,
Yet within, a fire burns within.

Crickets sing and owls take flight,
In the dark, there's pure delight.
The world transformed, an icebound glint,
In winter's grasp, our hearts imprint.

We gather 'round the fire's embrace,
Tales are shared, laughter has its place.
With flickers bright, the night stands still,
A magic spell, a winter thrill.

Silent Constellations of Frost

In the silence of night's hold,
Stars emerge like tales untold.
Frost adorns the earth below,
A tapestry of glimmering snow.

With every twinkle in the sky,
Dreams take flight and softly sigh.
The universe whispers secrets sweet,
Under the stars, time feels complete.

The chilly breath of night does creep,
As ancient myths from darkness leap.
Constellations weave their story,
In the stillness, of nature's glory.

We gaze up, hearts intertwined,
In this moment, souls aligned.
With fragile wonders overhead,
Silent wonders in dreams are fed.

As dawn approaches, shadows fade,
Yet in our hearts, the magic stayed.
Frost kisses the ground once more,
Silent constellations we adore.

Tranquility in Thaw

Gentle sun breaks through the frost,
Awakening the silent gloss.
Softly settles winter's sigh,
As the world begins to cry.

Melting whispers touch the ground,
Where the hidden blooms are found.
Nature stirs from frozen sleep,
In rhythms calm and sweet to keep.

Rippling streams begin to flow,
Bathed in warm and golden glow.
Every bud starts to expand,
Carrying spring's soft command.

Drifting clouds in azure dance,
Filling hearts with hope and chance.
In this moment, peace is nigh,
Underneath the clear, blue sky.

Quiet moments, life returns,
In our hearts, the spirit burns.
Tranquil thoughts like rivers glide,
As we welcome spring's sweet tide.

Faint Calls of Winter's Breath

In the hush of evening's light,
Whispers weave through fading night.
Crystals hang on barren trees,
Echoing the chilling breeze.

Voices soft as melting snow,
Winding where the shadows grow.
Each breath speaks of tales long gone,
In the twilight, winter's song.

Footsteps crunch on icy ground,
With playful echoes all around.
Nature's song, a haunting tune,
Underneath the silver moon.

In the distance, whispers rise,
Chasing dreams beneath the skies.
Faint calls of the night entwine,
In the stillness, hearts align.

Frosty patterns find their place,
Painting nature's frozen grace.
In this stillness, time remains,
While winter gently weaves its chains.

The Frigid Lullaby

Stars sprinkle the velvet night,
Cradled by the pale moonlight.
Winter's arms embrace so tight,
Singing softly, pure delight.

Chill winds whisper through the pines,
Nature's hush in sweet designs.
Every flake a note that falls,
In the night, as silence calls.

Snowflakes twirl like dreams above,
Gentle as a mother's love.
Crystalline, they kiss the ground,
In the stillness, peace is found.

Hushed beds of white emotions,
Rippling through the frozen oceans.
Wrapped in warmth, our thoughts take flight,
Falling into the silent night.

In this cradle of soft snow,
Beneath the moon's soft, watchful glow.
Winter sings its lullaby,
While the world waits, dreaming by.

Nightfall's Crystal Secrets

When the sun dips low and dies,
Stars awaken in the skies.
Wrapped in shades of deepening blue,
Night unfurls its secrets true.

Crystalline frost on every leaf,
Whispers softly of relief.
In this stillness, shadows creep,
Holding tight the dreams we keep.

Secret paths where moonlight glows,
Guide the heart where magic flows.
In the darkness, mysteries lie,
As the night begins to sigh.

Twinkling lights in nature's breath,
Breathe of life, yet hold of death.
Every glint reveals a tale,
In the night where echoes wail.

Underneath the starlit gaze,
Time suspends in moonlit haze.
Nightfall cradles all we seek,
In its arms, the world is meek.

Shadows of the Frosted Landscape

In the hush of winter's night,
Shadows dance in silver light.
Whispers weave through frozen pines,
Nature sings in icy lines.

Footprints trace a fleeting tale,
Underneath the moonlight pale.
Frosty breaths in twilight's gleam,
Awakening a silent dream.

Horizon kissed with shades of blue,
Each star twinkles, bold and true.
Crystals shimmer, soft and bright,
Echoing the hush of night.

Beneath the frost, old secrets lie,
Tales of snowflakes drifting by.
Every shadow holds a song,
Melodies from nights so long.

In this world of winter's grace,
Find your peace, your quiet place.
Let the shadows softly guide,
Through the whispers of the tide.

Solstice Secrets Beneath the Stars

Beneath the vast and velvet sky,
Solstice whispers gently sigh.
Stars align in cosmic dance,
Inviting hearts to take a chance.

Secrets wrapped in midnight's glow,
Silent dreams begin to flow.
Gravity of ancient light,
Pulling wishes through the night.

Each twinkle tells a story old,
Mysteries of life unfold.
In the silence, wisdom's gleaned,
Through the paths we've never dreamed.

Find your place among the gleam,
In a world of starlit dream.
Breathe in deep the twilight's grace,
And lose yourself in this embrace.

Moonlit shadows softly creep,
Filling hearts with tales to keep.
Solstice magic in the air,
Connected souls, beyond compare.

Ice-Kissed Musing of the Heart

Ice-kissed whispers brush the face,
Gentle feelings, boundless grace.
In the chill of winter's breath,
Lies a warmth that conquers death.

Musing on a love so rare,
Frosted petals, soft as air.
Silent vows in twilight's glow,
In the stillness, hearts will know.

Every tear that finds its way,
Turns to crystal, soft and gray.
Memories like snowflakes fall,
Each one echoing our call.

Underneath the frozen skies,
Hidden depth in fleeting sighs.
Ice-kissed dreams begin to thaw,
In their wake, a silent awe.

Let the heart be brave and bold,
As each story unfolds.
Tender moments, rich and sweet,
In this winter, we complete.

Veils of Glacial Sighs

Veils of ice upon the ground,
Whispers of the lost are found.
In the stillness, echoes dwell,
Tales of magic, stories swell.

Each breath leaves a mark in time,
Frosted air feels like a rhyme.
Glacial dreams that softly fall,
Touch the heart and heed the call.

Sighs that linger in the frost,
Remind us of what's gained and lost.
Nature's poetry, pure and free,
Wrapped in winter's mystery.

With each layer, truth unfolds,
Veils conceal what must be told.
In the depths of frozen night,
Love ignites the cold with light.

Let us wander through this space,
Finding warmth in frosted grace.
In the veils of glacial sighs,
Live the tales of snow's sweet cries.

Ethereal Touch of the Frigid Air

Whispers linger in the night,
A breath so soft, it takes its flight.
Gentle kisses from the sky,
The world enfolds in silence high.

Stars shimmer like frozen tears,
Echoes softly calm our fears.
With every gust, a song is played,
In winter's grasp, dreams are laid.

Frosted branches trace the moon,
Nature sings a crystal tune.
Each moment held in icy grace,
A fleeting dance, a soft embrace.

The world, a canvas painted white,
Illuminated by the light.
The air bites with a loving chill,
In every breath, a tranquil thrill.

We wander through this frozen scene,
Lost in thoughts of what has been.
With ethereal touch, the air does weave,
A tapestry of calm reprieve.

The Pulse of Subzero Serenity

In stillness lies a quiet beat,
A rhythm felt in snowy street.
Each heartbeat whispers, soft and low,
A pulse that guides us through the snow.

The trees stand tall, their branches bare,
Yet life persists in frozen air.
Subzero peace wraps round the day,
In shimmering light, dreams softly sway.

Evening falls, the world in peace,
From winter's grasp, we seek release.
Yet here within the icy glow,
Our hearts find warmth beneath the snow.

The quiet hum of night descends,
In cold embrace, the sadness mends.
Time drips like icicles down the eaves,
In silence woven, each heart believes.

With every breath, we feel the night,
The pulse of dreams in dimmed twilight.
Subzero serenity holds us near,
In the embrace of winter clear.

Lullabies of the Chill

Softly now, the night unfolds,
Cradled dreams in whispers bold.
Each breath a lullaby so sweet,
Guiding souls on silent feet.

The chill wraps round, a tender shawl,
A soothing balm for one and all.
White blankets hush the world in peace,
In frozen realms, the worries cease.

Crickets hush, the stars align,
Nature sings a lullaby divine.
Moonlight dances, shadows play,
As night gently slips away.

The frosty air, a gentle kiss,
In every corner, blissful bliss.
While winter's song fills up the sky,
We drift on waves of soft goodbye.

Through every chill, let heartbeats weave,
A tapestry of dreams believe.
In lullabies that winter spins,
Each tender note, a soul begins.

The Hush of Frozen Dawn

A quiet world beneath the frost,
In frozen light, our dreams are tossed.
The dawn breaks gently, soft and slow,
A canvas bathed in winter's glow.

With every breath, a silence deep,
The whispers of the night now sleep.
Snowflakes dance in morning's thread,
In quiet grace, the world is led.

Birds emerge, their songs refined,
A celebration, sweetly kind.
In this hush, we find a call,
To rise anew, to give our all.

The icy air, a fresh delight,
Awakens hearts with gentle might.
In frozen dawn, we start anew,
As warmth draws close, and skies turn blue.

So let the day unfold its charms,
Embrace the peace in nature's arms.
The hush of dawn, a tranquil balm,
In frozen moments, life feels calm.

The subtlest Touch of Ice

A whisper glides on frozen air,
Each breath a crystal, light and rare.
The world adorned in silver sheen,
A delicate dance, serene, unseen.

Frosted branches, silent plea,
Nature's art, pure harmony.
Glazed paths reflect the moon's soft glow,
An enchanted realm, where dreams flow.

The night embraces, cold and bright,
Stars twinkle in the frosty night.
Every flake a gentle touch,
A fleeting moment, oh so much.

With every step, the ice may crack,
Echoes of winter, no turning back.
Tender secrets in every freeze,
Life's quiet moments, meant to seize.

In this stillness, hearts unite,
Underneath the pale moonlight.
The subtlest touch of ice revealed,
A mystic beauty, forever sealed.

A Song of Snow and Stillness

The snowfall drapes a gentle quilt,
Nature's breath, all worries silt.
Each flake a note in winter's song,
Where silence reigns, and we belong.

Whispers of snowflakes in the night,
Twirl and dance, a pure delight.
Softly landing on limbs outstretched,
In this calm, our hearts are etched.

The trees stand tall, cloaked in white,
Guardians of dreams in soft twilight.
In the hush, time seems to freeze,
Moments captured with steady ease.

Footfalls muffled, secrets shared,
Every blink of stars declared.
Here in stillness, our spirits soar,
In the song of snow, we explore.

With every drift, a tale unfolds,
Ancient stories, quietly told.
A song of snow in the still night air,
Whispers of wonder, beyond compare.

Secrets Carved in Crystal

In icy depths, the secrets hide,
Where frozen whispers softly bide.
Carved in crystal, stories sleep,
Echoes of dreams, the silence keeps.

Glistening patterns, nature's scroll,
Each fracture holds a silent soul.
Under ice, the world is still,
Waiting, watching, time to fill.

Frigid light dances on the ground,
In every corner, magic found.
The cold caress, a lover's touch,
Promises linger, holding much.

With every gust, the secrets shift,
A tale untold, a precious gift.
Hours pass like snowflakes fall,
In this realm, there's space for all.

Embrace the stillness, breathe it in,
Let the crystal song begin.
Secrets carved in cold embrace,
In icy realms, we find our place.

Murmurs of the Winter Night

The winter night, a velvet cloak,
Where shadows dance and spirits evoke.
Moonbeams twinkle on drifts of snow,
Whispered secrets in the glow.

A breeze that sings through barren trees,
Carrying tales on icy breeze.
In every corner, stories spin,
Murmurs of nature, deep within.

Footsteps crunch on the frosty ground,
Each sound a heartbeat, softly found.
The world is hushed, a dream-like state,
In winter's grasp, we contemplate.

Stars shimmer bright in the frosty sky,
Painting wishes, as time drifts by.
Underneath this tranquil night,
Murmurs of magic take their flight.

So gather close, let the warmth ignite,
In each other's arms, we hold the light.
In whispers soft, the night will weave,
Murmurs of winter, hearts believe.

Echoes in the Ice

Whispers drift through frozen air,
Shadows dance without a care.
Ancient tales in silence spoken,
Memories wrapped in ice, unbroken.

Footsteps crunch on crystal ground,
In this stillness, peace is found.
Ghostly figures glide and weave,
Echoes linger, time to grieve.

In the depths of winter's chill,
Nature's heart beats soft and still.
Voices call from depths of white,
Guiding souls through endless night.

Stars above in velvet skies,
Glisten like bright, watchful eyes.
Moonlight bathes the world in grace,
Painting shadows, a silent place.

Yet beneath the icy sheen,
Lies a world, alive, unseen.
Through the echoes, one can hear,
Life persists, forever near.

Dances of a Winter Night

Snowflakes twirl in frosty glee,
Underneath the swaying tree.
Whispers join the frigid air,
Gentle movements everywhere.

Moonlight glides on silver streams,
Frosted branches hold their dreams.
In the hush where shadows lie,
Silent dances drift and sigh.

Winter whispers secrets old,
Tales of warmth in bitter cold.
Footsteps soft on icy trails,
As the heart of winter wails.

Stars begin their twinkling song,
Guiding souls who wander long.
In the night, magic's breath,
Embraces life, still as death.

Time slows down in this ballet,
Every moment feels like play.
On this night, the world feels light,
Dancing dreams in pure delight.

Chilling Reveries

Frosted windows, dreams take flight,
Canvas of a silent night.
Each breath forms a ghostly plume,
In the warmth of winter's room.

Chilling thoughts, sweet memories,
Wrapped in quilted histories.
Stories linger, soft and bright,
Echoes dance in pale moonlight.

Skating on a frozen lake,
Hearts collide with every break.
Underneath the starry dome,
Whispers call the heart back home.

Every flake a spark divine,
In the dark, we intertwine.
Laughter echoes through the frost,
In these moments, we are lost.

Veils of snow, a blanket wide,
Holding secrets deep inside.
Chilling reveries enfold,
In their grasp, we find the bold.

Secrets in the Frost

Beneath the frost, secrets sleep,
In stillness, thoughts begin to creep.
Winter's breath, a soft embrace,
Hiding magic in this place.

Icicles hang like whispered vows,
Nature bows with silent brows.
Each glimmer holds a hidden truth,
Wrapping youth in frost's own booth.

Footprints lead where shadows blend,
To a place where dreams extend.
Silence reigns, the world aligns,
In the cold, a warmth combines.

Berry red against the white,
Nature's palette, pure delight.
Secrets woven in the air,
In the frost, we find a prayer.

As the sun begins to rise,
Frosty gems become the prize.
In the light, the secrets born,
In every winter's quiet morn.

Hushed by the Snow

Blankets of white lay so still,
Softly they hush all the rills.
Whispers of quiet fill the air,
Nature's peace, beyond compare.

Footprints fade without a trace,
In this wonderland, time finds space.
Snowflakes dance with delicate grace,
In winter's soothing, cool embrace.

Branches bow with a frosty crown,
Each flake a jewel, gently falls down.
The world is draped in soft delight,
A tapestry woven, silent, bright.

Crimson berries peek through the frost,
In this tranquil realm, we find what's lost.
Hushed by the snow, the heart's refrain,
A moment captured, free from pain.

Beneath the sky, a silver glow,
All around is hushed by the snow.
In winter's hold, we breathe and sigh,
As dreams take flight, and time slips by.

Subtle Shimmers of Chill

Twilight blankets the world in gray,
Chill in the air begins to play.
Subtle shimmers catch the eye,
Stars awaken in the night sky.

Frosted whispers across the ground,
Magic of winter, softly found.
Crystals glisten, a silent song,
In the stillness, we feel we belong.

Moonlight dances on the frozen stream,
A world transformed, like a dream.
Every shadow tells a tale,
Of winter's magic, soft and pale.

Bare trees sparkle, their limbs aglow,
Nature's wonder, the dreams we sow.
As we walk through this chilly night,
Subtle shimmers bring delight.

In the distance, a hoot of an owl,
Echoing soft, like a gentle growl.
Wrapped in warmth under the sky,
Subtle shimmers, as time drifts by.

Secrets Beneath the Snow

Layers of white conceal the ground,
In silent peace, secrets are found.
Whispers of stories, old and new,
Beneath the snow, life continues.

Nature's blanket, soft and deep,
Holding the dreams that seek to keep.
Every flake a story untold,
In the winter's grip, treasures unfold.

Beneath the frost, a heartbeat lies,
Hope tucked away, where silence sighs.
Roots and seeds rest in quiet sleep,
Awaiting spring's call, promises to reap.

Snowdrifts swirl, the world fixed in time,
Each moment a secret, a silent rhyme.
As the sun warms the icy sheet,
Life awakens, strong and sweet.

With each thaw, the past reappears,
Unraveling stories, laughter, and tears.
Secrets beneath the snow will show,
Life's gentle cycle, a timeless flow.

The Soft Touch of Winter

Winter's breath brings a soft touch,
Whispers of cold that warm so much.
Gentle flakes fall like the lightest sigh,
Transforming the world as they float by.

A shimmered landscape, pure and bright,
Wrapped in silence, soft as night.
Each moment feels like a tender hold,
In winter's arms, a story told.

With every step, crunch beneath the boots,
Nature's rhythm in muted hoots.
The soft touch of frost on the face,
An invitation to find our place.

Candles flicker in the windows' glow,
Homes filled with warmth against the snow.
Hearts draw close to share the flame,
In winter's touch, we're never the same.

Wrapped in layers, cozy and right,
Embracing the magic of each night.
The soft touch of winter's grace,
A gentle reminder in time and space.

Winter's Silent Veil

Softly falls the snow at night,
Blanketing the world in white.
Silent whispers fill the air,
Nature rests, without a care.

Frosted branches bathe in light,
Stars twinkle through the quiet sight.
Dreams are held in winter's fold,
Tales of warmth from days of old.

Footsteps crunch on icy ground,
As the beauty wraps around.
Underneath the moon's embrace,
Winter's magic, a gentle space.

Frozen lakes, a mirror clear,
Reflecting all we hold so near.
In the stillness, hearts ignite,
Longing whispers through the night.

Candles flicker, shadows dance,
In winter's chill, we take a chance.
Wrapped in love, we share the glow,
Winter's silent veil, the world aglow.

Frigid Echoes at Dawn

Morning breaks with hues so pale,
Frosty breath on winter's trail.
Whispers of the night resign,
Frigid echoes so divine.

Sunrise paints the icy trees,
Shimmering in the softest breeze.
Silent songs of frosted air,
Nature wakes, beyond compare.

Footprints left in glistening snow,
Memories of the night's soft glow.
A distant bird takes to the sky,
Frigid echoes, sweet goodbye.

Cold embraces morning light,
Chill retreats from warming sight.
Life resumes with gentle grace,
Frigid echoes find their place.

As the sun begins to rise,
Winter dreams and nighttime ties.
In the dawn, a pure refrain,
A symphony of joy and pain.

The Breath of Ice

Whispers cold upon my face,
The breath of ice, a haunting grace.
Crystals form where shadows creep,
A frozen world lost in sleep.

Exhaling clouds of frosty air,
In this stillness, hearts can bare.
Nature's voice, both harsh and sweet,
In every flake, a tale complete.

Glacier's edge and mountain crest,
Silent creatures find their rest.
Hidden truths beneath the sheen,
The breath of ice where dreams convene.

Through frozen woods, we wander slow,
Each step a part of winter's flow.
Breath of ice, a chilling call,
Yet in its grasp, we feel it all.

Fires crackle in the night,
Warmth within, a fierce delight.
As winter holds the world so tight,
The breath of ice, a pure delight.

Chilled Whispers Beneath the Moon

Underneath the silver glow,
Chilled whispers dance with silent flow.
Stars align in velvet skies,
Nighttime secrets softly rise.

Winter's breath, a tender sigh,
Wraps the earth in a lullaby.
Crickets hush as shadows play,
In this magic, hearts will sway.

Moonbeams cast a gentle light,
Guiding souls through mystic night.
Frosty air, a kiss divine,
Chilled whispers, hearts entwine.

Every flicker, every sound,
Echoes linger all around.
In the quiet, dreams take flight,
Chilled whispers hold us tight.

As the night begins to wane,
Winter's beauty, none in vain.
In the stillness, love will bloom,
Chilled whispers beneath the moon.

Harmony in the Chill

In frosty air where silence reigns,
Nature breathes in soft refrains.
The world wrapped in a crystal coat,
A tranquil tune, a winter's note.

Branches bow beneath the weight,
Of glistening snow, a silent fate.
Harmony weaves through every tree,
A melody of peace, serene and free.

Footsteps crunch on frozen ground,
A symphony in each small sound.
While whispers dance on icy streams,
Reality stirs the softest dreams.

The sun peeks through, a golden light,
Turning the chill to warmth so bright.
Together they create a blend,
Of winter's wrath and warmth to mend.

Harmony sings in the quiet glow,
Of winter's grip, the beauty in snow.
Each flake a note, each gust a tune,
In this chilly haven, where heartbeats croon.

Echoes of the Snow-Laden Pines

Beneath the pines, the stillness sighs,
A hushed embrace of earth and skies.
Snowflakes fall like whispered dreams,
Blanketing the world in shimmering gleams.

Echoes linger among the trees,
Carried softly by the winter breeze.
Each branch adorned with frosted grace,
A serene beauty, a timeless space.

Footprints mark the trail we tread,
In the soft snow where stories spread.
Nature's canvas, a tale to unfold,
In the embrace of winter's cold.

Whispers dance on the frosty air,
Secrets shared with those who care.
In this quiet, a world reborn,
A peace that lingers, like the dawn.

Among the pines, our hearts unite,
In echoes soft, in purest light.
Winter's charm, a gentle art,
In the snow-laden woods, we are a part.

Hushed Footprints

In the stillness of the night,
Soft snowflakes fall, a pure delight.
Hushed footprints linger in the frost,
Mapping paths of what was lost.

The moon casts shadows, pale and bright,
Guiding dreams through the sparkling white.
Each step a whisper, a gentle trace,
Through winter's cold, a warm embrace.

Frosty breath hangs in the air,
A fleeting moment, a silent prayer.
Connecting souls with every stride,
In this quiet world, we abide.

Gentle winds stir the silent night,
Carrying wishes in their flight.
In hushed footsteps, secrets are found,
Echoes of love all around.

With every imprint in the pure snow,
Stories linger, hearts aglow.
In the stillness where we tread,
The world awakens, softly spread.

Whispers of the Glacie

Beneath the azure skies so clear,
The glaciers whisper stories near.
Ancient tales of time and space,
In icy depths, they leave their trace.

Cracks and creaks, the voice of frost,
Reminding us of what is lost.
Each shimmer holds a sunlit dream,
Reflections dance in the icy stream.

The world beholden to their grace,
Frozen beauty in a solemn place.
Carved by time, they stand so tall,
Guardians of secrets, they hold all.

Whispers echo across the land,
A haunting song, a gentle hand.
With every glimmer, a breath of chill,
The glacier's heart beats, still and still.

Among the whispers, hope does rise,
Promising tomorrows beneath the skies.
Through ice and time, we seek to know,
The whispers of the glacie, softly flow.

Glistening Mirrors of a Frosty Night

In the moon's gentle glow, light does beam,
Snowflakes dance freely, a beautiful dream.
Each crystal reflects a story untold,
Glistening mirrors, in silver and gold.

Whispers of winter weave through the trees,
A soft, silent symphony carried by breeze.
Nature's canvas, a splendid display,
Painted with frost, still as a ballet.

Stars twinkle down, a watchful delight,
Casting their wishes on this frosty night.
With each breath exhaled, a misty plume,
Fragile and fleeting, in winter's cool gloom.

A tranquil embrace, the world holds its breath,
As shadows of night cradle dreams of the breadth.
In this frozen moment, time seems to stall,
A serene celebration, enchanting us all.

Glistening wonders, winter's parade,
Mirrored reflections, memories laid.
In the chill of the night, all worries take flight,
In the heart of the frost, we find our delight.

The Whispering Wind's Touch

Through whispering leaves, the wind creeps low,
Carrying secrets only it can know.
A gentle caress, on skin warm and bare,
Nature's soft touch, without a single care.

With each rustle, stories awaken anew,
Tales of the ancients that once breezed through.
Life's gentle caress, both soothing and wild,
In its embrace, we feel eternally beguiled.

The scent of the earth, rich and profound,
In the breath of the wind, solace is found.
It wisps around corners, offering grace,
A fleeting kiss upon nature's face.

Clouds soar above, carried high in the sky,
The whispers grow bold, as the sun says goodbye.
Encircling the world with its rhythmic hum,
The wind sings a lullaby, inviting us home.

In the quiet of night, when all seems still,
The wind still wanders, its mission to thrill.
With every soft stir, it beckons us near,
A timeless reminder that nature is here.

Echoing Dreams of Ice

In the silence of frost, dreams begin to play,
Echoing softly with the light of day.
A canvas of white where whispers reside,
Unfolding each moment, like a shimmering tide.

With each fragile flake that the chilly winds blow,
A story is woven, a beautiful flow.
Echoes of laughter, locked in the freeze,
As hearts warm together, seeking to please.

Under the stars, the world feels so vast,
In dreams dipped in ice, we escape the past.
A dance of reflections upon the pure night,
Where hope and desire take graceful flight.

The shimmering crystals, each one a spark,
Ignite the dark sky, illuminating the stark.
In this quiet expanse, where time softly sighs,
Each heartbeat is echoed, as the cold softly cries.

In the grip of the freeze, our dreams intertwine,
As ice forms the stage, and our spirits align.
In this enchanted realm, we find our true voice,
Echoing dreams of ice, where we all rejoice.

Chilling Tranquility

A hush blankets all, in the stillness of night,
Chilling tranquility, a beautiful sight.
Frost holds its breath, under a blanket of stars,
Whispers of peace, like the moonlight that spars.

Shadows stretch long, with the sun's soft retreat,
Nature holds close, all the moments so sweet.
In the crispness of air, clarity glows,
Chilling tranquility, where calmness flows.

Each twinkle above, tells a story of old,
Of time gently passing, both timid and bold.
As night deepens softly, dreams quietly unfold,
Wrapped in serenity, vibrant and cold.

Silent reflections in the mirror-like lake,
Hope dances gently, no heart left to break.
Amidst quietude, peace takes its reign,
Chilling tranquility, washing away pain.

In the stillness, we breathe, and time becomes free,
In this haven of calm, we are meant to be.
Wrapped in the silence, the cold feels so right,
Embracing the chill in the soft, tender night.

A Breath of Ice

In the hush of dawn, a whisper flows,
Chilling depths where the soft wind goes.
Crystal breath upon the ground,
Nature's stillness, a peace profound.

Frosted branches bow and sway,
Carrying secrets of the frigid day.
Veils of white on rooftops gleam,
A world captured in a frozen dream.

Footprints fade in the silver dust,
Under skies so bright, so just.
The air bites with an icy kiss,
A fleeting moment of wintry bliss.

As daylight fades, shadows creep,
Wrapped in silence, the earth now sleeps.
Each breath released in a cloud of grey,
Whispers of winter drift away.

Awake the night, the moon will rise,
Reflecting light in frozen skies.
A breath of ice, a gentle plea,
As nature dreams in tranquility.

Shards of Winter Silence

Beneath the weight of snowflakes' fall,
A brittle hush envelops all.
Shards of silence thick and deep,
Guarding secrets that winter keeps.

Trees stand tall in their icy shrouds,
Casting shadows in shimmering clouds.
Every corner, a crystal glow,
Nature's magic, simple and slow.

Footsteps echo on the frozen ground,
In solitude, the heart is found.
A breath, a pause, the world holds tight,
In shards of winter, pure delight.

As twilight sets the sky ablaze,
The stars emerge from their hidden maze.
A chilly breeze sings through the night,
Wrapped in wonder, a world of light.

With every breath, the cold ignites,
Awakening dreams in frosty sights.
In the stillness, a tale unfolds,
Shards of winter, stories told.

Twinkling in the Cold

The frosty air, a crisp embrace,
Reflecting light in every place.
Twinkling stars, they dance and weave,
Over landscapes that winter leaves.

Silvery fog blankets the earth,
Whispers of magic, laughter, and mirth.
Each flicker tells of nights long past,
Memories held in cold shadows cast.

In the stillness, hearts ignite,
With hopes that shimmer in the night.
As we gather under the sky,
Warmth of love will never die.

A cozy fire, a beacon's glow,
As outside the gentle breezes blow.
Twinkling in the cold, we share,
The bonds of family, love, and care.

With every toast, the spirits rise,
Filling the room with laughter and sighs.
Together we shine, a guiding light,
In the twinkling cold, our hearts are bright.

Ethereal Freeze

Time stands still in the frosty air,
An ethereal freeze beyond compare.
Each flake a jewel, each breath a song,
In this winter's cradle where dreams belong.

Glistening fields stretch wide and far,
Under the gaze of a watchful star.
Nature sparkles in a silvery veil,
Whispers of wonder in every trail.

The quiet hum of a world at peace,
In the chill, the noise will cease.
Moments sway like branches bare,
Ethereal visions dance in the air.

Beneath the moon's soft, luminescent glow,
Life carries on beneath the snow.
Each heartbeat echoes, strong and true,
In the ethereal freeze, I find you.

A fleeting dream, a time well spent,
Wrapped in serenity, no need to lament.
Ingredients of joy in winter's embrace,
Ethereal freeze, our timeless space.

A Palette of Winter Breath

In cool hues, the world awaits,
A canvas white, where silence sates.
Frosty whispers, soft and light,
Dance in the shadows, take their flight.

Barren branches, lace entwined,
Nature's song, a muted find.
The chill wraps tight, the night draws near,
A palette painted, crystal clear.

Echoes of joy, beneath the glow,
Of twinkling stars all draped in snow.
Winter's breath, a gentle sigh,
Breathes life into the starlit sky.

Crisp air carries winter's call,
A silent promise, embracing all.
Each flake a story, pure delight,
Unfolding magic through the night.

And then the dawn, a golden spark,
Illuminates the frozen park.
With every step, the world will gleam,
In winter's grasp, we pause and dream.

The Shy Glimmer of Snow

The sky adorned in shades of gray,
Whispers secrets of winter's play.
A shy glimmer starts to fall,
In gentle flurries, soft and small.

Each flake a wish, a silent prayer,
Crafted with love, spun from the air.
They dance quietly, a tender race,
Embracing earth in a cold embrace.

Footprints mark the snowy ground,
A fleeting echo, barely sound.
Nature holds her breath with grace,
As time slows down in this sacred space.

Branches bow with weighty lace,
Glistening softly, a sweet embrace.
In this hushed world, our hearts will twine,
With the shy glimmer of snow's design.

As night descends, the stars appear,
Casting warmth despite the chill near.
In stillness, dreams begin to grow,
Wrapped in the beauty of winter's glow.

Unseen Frost in the Night

A whisper waits in shadows deep,
Where unseen frost begins to creep.
It blankets dreams with soft caress,
In silver hints of quietness.

The moonlight bathes the silent street,
A symphony, the night feels sweet.
Each breath released in chilly air,
Carries thoughts of warmth and care.

Underneath the blanket white,
The world slumbers, filled with light.
Stars twinkle soft, a gentle guide,
Through winter's realm, we magic abide.

Every glimmer, a tale untold,
Of unseen frost, a sight to behold.
It sparkles lightly, a hidden treasure,
Bringing comfort, peace, and pleasure.

As dawn approaches, colors rise,
Melting whispers, the night complies.
Yet remnants of that secret night,
Hold memories in dawn's first light.

The Hidden Chime of Winter's Breath

In the stillness, a chime resounds,
Through icy air, it gently bounds.
The hidden notes of winter's song,
Awake the hearts that have waited long.

Each breath a melody, crisp and clear,
Calls us forth to bring us near.
Nature's voice, soft and meek,
Whispers secrets, beauty speaks.

Frosted leaves, like diamonds glow,
Beneath the weight of soft white snow.
Each step a sound, a heart's embrace,
Echoing with the fleeting grace.

The chill caresses as twilight sways,
A quiet beauty that always stays.
In the hush of night, we find our peace,
Where winter's breath will never cease.

Awakening senses, the spell we weave,
In awe of the gifts that winter leaves.
The hidden chime will always play,
Through frosty nights to break of day.

Twilight's Breath in Ice

As twilight descends, the shadows grow,
A whisper of frost begins to flow.
Glistening edges, the world turns bright,
Embraced by the chill of the coming night.

The air grows still, in silence we stand,
Holding the magic of winter's hand.
Frost on the petals, a delicate trace,
Twilight's breath in this frozen space.

Stars twinkle softly in the darkening sky,
Breath mingles like mist as we stand by.
Nature's embrace in a cold, tender way,
Awakens the heart at the close of the day.

The moon casts its glow on the snowy ground,
In this chill embrace, true peace is found.
Dreams intertwine with the crystal clear night,
As twilight whispers, embracing the light.

Frozen echoes of laughter and song,
In this moment, we truly belong.
Time halts in beauty, a scene sublime,
Twilight's breath in this frosty thyme.

Chasing Adrift Snowflakes

Snowflakes drift softly, a dance in the air,
Swirling and twirling without a care.
Chasing their paths as they flutter and glide,
Each one unique as they tumble and slide.

Laughter erupts in the chill of the morn,
Catching the flakes as they're gently borne.
Their icy kiss upon a warm cheek,
Moments like diamonds, special and unique.

A symphony plays with each fall and rise,
Nature's sweet magic, a joyful surprise.
Whispers of winter surround us with glee,
Chasing adrift snowflakes, just you and me.

Timeless we wander in this frosty embrace,
Casting our wishes through delicate space.
With arms open wide, we leap and we spin,
Embracing the chill that draws us all in.

These fleeting moments, like snow on the ground,
Ephemeral beauty, so easily found.
Chasing adrift snowflakes, we revel in light,
In the wonder of winter, our hearts take flight.

Glimmers of Hidden Chill

In the stillness of dawn, secrets unfold,
Glimmers of frost like stories once told.
Each spark on the grass, a moment in time,
Whispering softly, a delicate rhyme.

Beneath the pale sun, a shimmer of ice,
Every breath taken feels splendidly nice.
Nature awakes with a frosted embrace,
Glimmers of hidden chill blend beauty with grace.

Crystal reflections dance in the light,
Each glimmer a promise, a breathtaking sight.
The world wrapped in silver, a mystical hue,
Glimmers appearing, revealing what's true.

Time flows like water, yet stops in this space,
Capturing moments, a tender chase.
Each glimmer ignites a spark in the heart,
Hidden chill offers a chance for new start.

With tracks softly laid in the powdery snow,
Glimmers of hidden chill let magic grow.
Together we wander, lost in this thrill,
In the tender embrace of winter's sweet chill.

Frosted Paths of Memory

Through frosted paths where the old stories lie,
Each step we take makes the past come alive.
Footprints of laughter, shadows of light,
Frozen in time as we journey through night.

Whispers of winters long gone fill the air,
Echoes of friendship linger everywhere.
Carved in the snow, every moment we share,
On these frosted paths, memories repair.

With each gentle breath, we savor the chill,
Reliving the magic, a moment to fill.
The cold wraps around us like a worn shawl,
Frosted paths beckon, we answer their call.

Mornings of wonder, the sun paints the skies,
Awakening feelings and softening sighs.
Together we tread through the frost and the snow,
In the warmth of our hearts, the memories flow.

These paths may be cold, but they lead us to light,
Frosted reflections, a beautiful sight.
Together we wander where memories dwell,
In frosted paths of memory, we'll always tell.

Veils of Cold Whispers

In shadows deep, the whispers sigh,
A shiver courses through the night.
Veils of cold, they softly fly,
As moonlight drapes the world in white.

Ghostly echoes in the breeze,
Tickling the ears of the trees.
Stories spun with every freeze,
Nature's song, a hush that frees.

The silent dance of frost and time,
In each breath, a verse, a rhyme.
Chilled by winter's softest chime,
A melody so pure, sublime.

Underneath the starlit dome,
Whispers call, a heart's lost home.
With every step, where shadows roam,
Veils of cold, no longer alone.

As dawn approaches, light will break,
And with it, warmth the frost will shake.
Yet in the night, for now, we wake,
To veils of whispers, memories make.

Frozen Petals Falling

Upon the ground where petals lie,
In shades of white, the blooms now cry.
Frozen whispers from the sky,
A brief embrace, then drift on by.

Beneath the frost, the garden sleeps,
In silent dreams, the secrets keep.
Nature's heart, so still, it weeps,
For beauty lost, as winter creeps.

When icy winds embrace the air,
Each fragile petal, lost to care.
Yet in this chill, there lies a flare,
Of memories sweet, beyond compare.

The world transformed, like muted art,
A canvas blank, a fresh new start.
From frozen depths, life shall depart,
And spring will mend a broken heart.

In time, the thaw will surely come,
And with it, life, a gentle hum.
Yet still, for now, the silence drums,
As frozen petals succumb to numb.

The Sound of Frost

A crackling hush, the world asleep,
Where icy fingers gently creep.
In every breath, the secrets keep,
The sound of frost, a whispered leap.

Through barren woods, the echoes roam,
A chilling song, the heart feels home.
With every sound, the stillness combs,
As nature hums its winter poem.

The crunch beneath a footstep's tread,
A fleeting moment, where thoughts are led.
In frozen stillness, dreams are bred,
A dance of whispers, softly spread.

The world adorned in crystal guise,
Reflections caught in silvered eyes.
With every sound, a soft surprise,
As moonlight bathes the night in lies.

Yet soon the thaw will draw us near,
To warmer days, where hearts conquer fear.
But for this night, let frost appear,
As echoes hush, the world sincere.

Muffled Footfalls in Snow

In soft embrace, the snowflakes fall,
Muffled whispers to nature's call.
Each footstep bears a gentle thrall,
As winter's spell weaves over all.

The silence thick, a blanket white,
Steps taken slow in soft moonlight.
Each crunch a note, a sweet delight,
In winter's arms, we find our flight.

Beneath the pines, the shadows play,
Tracing paths where wanderers stray.
The spark of night, the dawn's decay,
Muffled footfalls, love's ballet.

In every twist of snowy lane,
Memories form in frost and grain.
We carve our tales, like soft refrains,
In whispered moments, joy and pain.

Soon spring will break the spell we know,
But for tonight, let silence flow.
Muffled footfalls in the snow,
Marking paths where lovers go.

Milton Keynes UK
Ingram Content Group UK Ltd.
UKHW010231111224
452348UK00011B/681